marginal utility

marginal utility

Tracey McTague

marginal utility by Tracey McTague
Published by Trembling Pillow Press
New Orleans, LA
ISBN-13: 9781732364738
Copyright © 2019 Tracey McTague

All Rights Reserved. No part of this book may be reproduced in any form without permission from the publisher with the exception of brief passages cited or for educational purposes. Reproduction for commercial use is prohibited except by permission of the author.

Typesetting and Design: Megan Burns
Cover Design: Matthew Revert
Cover Art: Mike Joyce
Copyedit: Kia Alice Groom
Interior Chapter Art: Chris Ando

NEW ORLEANS

for
Aurora Morrigan

marginal utility

Mule:
blueprint of the yoke

demirep per diem

*"The furcula, or wishbone, evolved to strengthen
the skeleton of birds to withstand the rigors of flight."*

synchronicity   in our little deaths
feeling your molecules   the size of buckeyes
      dwelling inward in tattoo invocation
flâneur fox to raven transcendence
by way of mule's clumsy heart
tethered with intrepidity
to yoked fusion   an echo   in succumbed radiance
a sum of rays conjured into wing – hoof & paw
to push swaddled clouds apart

there's far too much sky in your eye
for mouth-blossom's rampant weeds
our wormhole abundance overflow
of nape & rising star perfervid
in coven of three
with fire worn inside out
to consummate wishbone
this thing of ours   plunges infinite
into all ye need to know
our vice versed in this
& dying to arrive
ravenous with dervish

fetish of bread & roses
branded onto back
in obscure divinities of light

cephalopod & cephalophore

inhabit heyday forevermore
exegete of ecstatic
small mercies found in scant shadow
to be rapt-sublime & born to contraries
with oxytocin for Orwellian observations
a mammalian novelty of djellaba lingerie
masking more true unveils
Joe Hill's g-spot

cartography of truffle hunters'
pheromone memoir
possesses this flood of being
& throbbing glow of low sun
for a dark lady's noisy heart

flankstrap
for Davis

"It dawns on me that I did not know what I knew:
my best friend's nose."
Taken from Degas' note to Valéry, sent in the petit-bleu.

a mind of its own

a cornerstone of glory & decline

more bull than fighter

provisional space inhabited

by simulacra cinema's subplot

contingently coiled in domestic drama

with empathy for mule skinners'

intention on the jerk line

in time machine de jour

colonizing divide sways

transcendent moments

in samhain-lackey mule

A mule is always a stranger. You never know the heart of them.

unflappable agony or not

eat the meat off their bones

& transform them to specter

ghosted out into tidal current of schmaltz

lost by a nose

trompe l'oeil

*"Some of us wanted a piece of the pie,
and some of us wanted to blow the whole pie up."*

dove pie Armageddon
become your own cliché
into rivers infinite flow
while collecting paradise
one stink horn at a time
crepuscular ghost moths
seen at oblique angles
as lugubrious light lingered
lux et veritas – 24 frames later
with a grudge for agrarian virtue
& an ear for syncopation
echo controposto immortal
infinity bursting forward from Venus-hip
always forever now foretelling
another bad day in the empire

riding horses on ruined highways

belief in omens   in the wake of storms
elicits sibyl slip-up & takes a cake walk
with crows' casual divination of flight
down a blind alley   right up mine

perfidies last hewn gleam of horrible hope
thrill & dread beneath sclera cues
wondering where's *my* taco at?
in the shadow of naysayers'
punched-in-the-face kind of kiss
ripe   in our wilderness   gone

aqua regia (river opus)

before fence & minced oaths masked
in juke joint's last dance
lunar-tics of gatherers
& betrayed brood mare's blood
lingua franca's scarred savants
heed these   the rules of starved wolves

deviant martyrs mark the days
under bloodied sky
a river rolls with the punch's drunk yoke
workhorse tuned to G
hallowed & exquisitely remote
knowing the river forgets
euphoric in coyote corpse

nom vaillant

"it's just a hand," she said
throw the dice
rending pulse anew
in rando hawkmoth flyby
bird-hip-trick unfolds
from grasping to flight
jou m lonje
for divine twin & boreal songbird
throw the knucklebone game
kundalini unicorn
our hives as humiliating as desire
so lavishly layered & lost to next day's light
with honey tongue's lilting field
of vision drowning in excess
in primal directive
all awash in nerve
beyond restless sea wall
& permeate forgotten unknowns
straight as a die
roots without end
rolled into Mississippi memento

humbucker most nigh

"Snake farm, it just sounds nasty, well, it pretty much is."

something akin to vision being heard
in memoria of absolutes in absentia
gone again moreover
just ocean at the end of sweet berth's
captured sum of rays – light in play
our vaulted echoes in radiance bond

guitar patina of woodworn suffering
a remarkable crow knows to be angry at the sun
our continuum for future yesterday's
shifting singularities
& obtains writ for piano practice
a fortune teller typo
written backwards on our palms

sophists at dinner

retinal art reject
home to roost in roar
permit yourself this sky
seeded hope renders merciless
nobodies with collateral make-outs
& obliterate your operatives
we never existed
acrostics aplenty but defunct
in ballpark of eternity's
intro to intricacies
anarchy's bona fide ride
in terrarium transcendence
while people walked on the moon

pithy bits omitted
in wrap-it-up summit
quirks below the belt
suss out doom riff
in ephemera endgame
Duchamp's indexed ricochet
& portrait as landscape

courtesan tendencies in an epoch of degeneration

sacred Virgin-Whore in bas relief
step into my war room & tell me where it hurts
your spore-born shadow succinctly swells
into devotees of John the Conqueror Root
given freely to plasma guitar
defying magnificent tendencies for charm quota
while the blood was warm yet
trickling over us holding court
on porch until the end of the adventure
for sale with calculated abandon
for all our dead fathers & their wives
with particular attachments
to textured layers of harlotry
her salamander universe getaway gets away
in confessions of a poet
that loved unwisely well
into realms resurrective for birds on fire
bristle under divine punishment
drop mask & prepare spirit
for Josie Arlington's grave
smelling like candy & rage in here
Animist pulse beholden
will generally ruin you
consecrated to bliss & loss
the lady on the first floor
tête-à-tête scandal of want

with particular attachments
pecuniary view full of spirits
& a house for every desire

nom de guerre

one habitué of the place
a former demimonde scalawag
with weekly douceurs left discreetly
for those who hustled
walking in champagne
with Irish Channel snitch
& erstwhile office clerk
a shadow of former selves
just *the girl next door*
in the age of shift drinks
& lagniappe in your cap
double whammy's – road to nowhere
opens up to everything
in this not-so-promised land
our mosey walk apocalypse
hushed conspiracy of the empirical
living elsewhere shattered
somewhere in between
our undressed code
on permanent sabbatical
proselytize perchance
this flesh & blood
& forgive my malapropisms
battling bored gods
& hungry with patois fiasco
a masked deflection

of shared scotopia
our many tongues shortlisted
& abducted by waxing caveat
the fever of life – still in the blood
busking evermore

held in a song

looming loom strung out and strung upon
woman as ornament in Hades sidecar
miracles made easy with standard sleights
of hand & various illusions
Penelope's halls filled up
tributes made in dream visions
in the melee's appalling spectacle
phantom pregnancy birthed between phantom limbs
panhandling cosmic origin
& intractable endings
brain threaded through
cherished model of world
with standard gravity & apathy
intermission capsized
backwards thirst
words hardly immense enough
dissipation & much slang expended
in the flower of their age
reliably computed
aboard ships - mortals avant!
indebted to snakes abreast
goddesses & other forgotten histories

anodynes anonymous

momentarily alone in your thoughts
while you muddle cocktails
in the skulls of the 1%
more lint found   than thread lost
on the convergence of two rivers
catfishing yourself
as uncontained as possible
in leitmotif reservoir
drifting melody heard through ceiling
our dream corridors opening up again
& cape jasmine in your lap

Mississippi appendectomies

still seaworthy & populated by vivid disappointments
glorious wreck of rot
pilloried memories & shadows
but still worth her salt

caress spectral strands of oblivion
light a candle for wombs
& transitional objects
our torrid decrepitude's idiom
found in defiant gaze
of daguerreotype nude
theme in between
loss & limerence notes
damned if she does & damned if she does nothing
in galaxies of lesser import

Delta Donuts

sign in donut shop reads: 0 bedrooms   vacant land   home
angels of our nature getting their share
& our cocksure nemesis coalesces into whole
light lost in bits of dialogue
but slow plot implode often besides the point
genre flick's third-rail come-on
for topless dancer at Delta Donuts
second sight in two fold twilight
double your money with double vision
formulaic foreplay foreshadows
sublimely shallow
lately it's been so   whatever
gerrymandered jubilee
left rare beasts wary
in a smaller cadenza
instincts curdled into suspicion
in embryonic detail
mordant shadow fever
my rooms all died
with solitude flotsam
add zest of vulgar rind
meandering & already lost
redemptive wing tattoo
in standards of the lucky cigarette   all that's left

Kitsuné:
escape of the flâneur

raven paradox
"Fucking was my Beatrice."

the raven is what we do next
mono no aware
on the face of it
flesh out flesh in fox-skin shed
for threshold identities
of sumptuous algorithms
bequeathed to snake revelator
this bootless bird of daybreak
dark flight thwarts ingrate sun again
brain oeuvre annealed
our temporary forms glimpsed
while opening the hand of thought
for oracle corvid in rapture
unbroken wing transcends us

homecoming queen   turned nothing

optima dies prima fugit

it was her habit to play the horses	succumb to fancy dressing
& roam with desperate characters	raised with alligators
as a sideline	she was a procuress of secrets
not long in one place	*"Better to die on the wing!"*
crows circled above her	fading plague of flesh
& burdened your eye	with corvid inklings
at séance of aborted beignets	into periphery of shadow
feathers plucked from hands	on broken saints
under derby day ladders	the luck didn't hold
wanting what it wants	horses shot again

            to blaspheme another year

lingua ignota

quantum world trafficked
into fox's perpetual unweaving of self
adorned in hyacinth
& mirror still shadowed by split self
through a series of disgusts
girl   you got Soloed   — I know I know

sensations dissolved in mist
omitted landscape & continual vanishing
of fallen shrouds & gleaming intervals
it's too much beauty to stand   in your shattered hand
those glorious atoms   made in the furnace of long dead stars
extending beyond shade — iron rusts and fruit ripens
far out on every side
gesturing toward the condition of music
& the constant effort to obliterate it

Yali's Cargo Bar
for Anselm

crow saint of sky without future
without time prisoner of splendor & pain
so many more particles than anti particles
non quantum explanation & conversations with future self
writing guidebook to the worst places on earth
making wishes on neutron stars
a ring of anti matter will have to do
ghost of no pivots to its past
it's in you
trapped in an orbit
supported against future collapse
amused bandit of past selves
pain is just an interpretation of the brain
flesh bleeding a story today
of a girl slipping out of her skin on cue
alighting on dead trees
she told me to stop putting out the fires
these forests are made to burn
smoldering illumination of absence
tomb-radiant apple-seeded Eden
with heirs & feudal fox
still seen in dreams
& no one can hear you scream in space

boundless detour

yegg's pulled punches
for atonal wilds in exiled constraint
these poison kernels in my control theory
all of us   homeland vagabonds
chained blood hounds finding solace
ripe for looting jealousy's tin foil hat
another thing to unravel into ruin
& doom the whole enterprise
beneath is the game afoot
in suburb of cul-de-sacs
& desire machines of coochie cabals
make me a pallet   soft & low
our movie is part noir & mostly octopus
& the real reason cartoon bears are pantless

cipher libre

arcanum of adept's secret rites
longing in the vitals
for abhaya mudra's fingerfuck syntax
& overflow into ordinary

prefer not to see pixels
conjured by knowing the ending
on brink of water
opened up to empty ocean at the end
mermaid's taxonomy
& lumpers lost to splitters again
ogle opens eye & consumes chrysalis
axis of complicit pelvis
boundary lost itself to blood aloft
in D-sharp minor of feather apogee
configured to home-vector
with opaque mirror as identity pastiche

quantum entanglement

haze & lurid glow of cityscape
the germs of empires
for interloper bearing sword
& vanishes into flat farm horizon
imagine the very end in this monstrous place

Metaire cemetery lights reflect
a secret not worth knowing
keep it under your hat while speaking through it
apathy always smells of lies and decay
in the throes of love or rigor mortis
I'll drink to you and your new tattoo

save your soul with octopus and other blessed devils
architecture of harness yielding a beacon
for working stiff tethered
to pink deeper than silver
an evening in any house
cost you just as much
as you had in your pocket
four quarters for piano
two dollar bill for the women
two dollar bill for the wine
50 cents for "extras"
under a storm washed unicorn

as for the carcass
we wasted nothing
guilded veins dying a little every day
for construct's terrible hindsight
everything less strange than ever

Notes From the Numbing Room
for John Godfrey

"He was awake a long time before he remembered his heart was broken."

Orpheus invents duende
for the flamenco mad Maenads   (not Eurydice)
it is the same death eternally
spontaneous human combustion
"She is too fine to be my wife," Mr. Cleary said
eternal sound of looking back
a veritable torrent of newts in a fever dream
flame bursts from mother's mouth
almost a cinder   swept into ceaseless shadow
& faces burdened with light
fluent in unhinged auger
& that reoccurring dream of buying milk
at the hardware store

anchor in a flood epoch
for J.A.S.

it's all sky now
in the sweet fête
by & bye   pie times behind us
in this land of selfie-stick opiate
& Dunbar's number one friend
happily drowned in this ardent expanse
even in more vertical moments
language nascent & subject to sweet corruption
in sun streaked sublime
this bird with Sanskrit heartbeat
finds home out of nothing
born like this with breakneck devotion
craving truth like air to flourish up
& sing into my mouth
with patois of redemption
& neck musk vipassanā
BTW: forearms are obscene
Brooklyn, Beirut, Bobigny
places to inhabit life everyday
in any vein of your body
with rub board's porch percussion
& 2 dollar bill's emissary of pity
under the wreck of my sweater
my skandhas miss your skandhas

amore y amaro

"the darkest place is always under the lamp"

brief sense of startling hope
while sky goes grey
the guise of tomorrow etched on a transom
her small figure obliterated by light
cook the hen that doesn't lay
pursuing the oracles
of exquisite grotesque
chronicle of dark woods
in glimpsed light

amuse louche
Furcula Borealis, a moth attracted to light and decay

kyōsaku with ball gag
after edible underwear recall
twofold emergence from shadow-eon
freshly coppered & almost perfect
let wound bleed out
dead ends dead ahead
creatures of habit inhabit the hunt
chronicle of desired cast-offs
cryptic tableau takes back the hat
for my life coach's skull device
in ancient heresies reinvented as self-help
numbing as best as can be
skeleton crew leveraging plow perils
for ghosts in modular homes
purging these damned bones galore
when grace is lost

le paradis des orages s'effondre
for Brett Evans's birthday on All Saints' Day

whence
    paradise of storms
        endlessly for an hour
phantoms reverted to exile   meet again
hardly sneering this time   secondhand song's
fanfare turned back   by blacklight owl
vévé shuts up voluptuous   in super storm absentia's
end of the world report   arise in remade vein
call-dropped   vs.   drop-kicked
in pastiche grief   &   sabotage collage
these lost provinces   après nous
    le deluge

elysian excess

tethered heart's thirsty tenure
suckled by wolf-dog-scabs
the pale fence beyond
mortification of varied veils
inlaid with peacock
in pristine hotel rooms unrequited
& post card's complicity with absence
erasure as mural
an alligator ate another alligator
without remorse today
glass door's fractured mosaic
in light invocation
for Wonder Wheel doula
breaking the horns apart

devil in the details

for Jim Behrle

field guide to American houses
plays a worried note wrapped in twelve bars
slurred truth be told in erasure
forced over major key
keening slide in degrees
your 'life is short' shirt worn thin
into color of ash or half inked stamp
ichneumon's trade of replenished self
& deism from caterpillar hollow
for proto pilgrim's witch uplifted
& whale tail's terrestrial trick
of larval-go-between
somewhere between a boner & crying
vestigial limbs become irrelevant
with annointed poet spyhole
into afterhour paint-by-number club
subsiding subplots for suburban wife-swap
& anarchy's itch fixed by birds of paradise folio
pre history's pale crow & arrant thief of sun
your tail came up heads again

Ní fhanann trá le fear mall
for Nora
(The tide does not wait for the slow man.)

in dumb silence everywhere
utopia fled hope into conquered sky
dreaming of a story already taken place
words smoothed into nothingness
Yes *(apparently)* is a feminine word
voluptuous fetish of death in tidal ebb
enter vixen lair profaned
with bones of farm plunder
agreeable boundary obliged
to employ your breath deficiency
in caged bird's rising notes
echoed in ruined city lulled to sleep
with eyes wide open & desires distant
never born but daily sold
changeling wives wade into deep
"… out to sea with you woman."
become virtuouso spirit
freed by lack of breath
& mitigate this jet vein yet

dowse a double life

"This is a token."

coyote   never look down
under semi-detached-brickface
mugging for mugshot (*yipe again*)
with free mocktails at pregnancy bar's soft opening
as grackles on a roll gate wait out the rain
nestled in sluggish nightmare of everyday
walk the perimeter soldier
call of the civilized from a banker named Buck
we're all lost in the exclusion zone
fallout shelter rust
F-sharp echo undercurrent
& other problems of hope

night of the hunter

for Brendan Lorber

under first snow   sky cluttered here   & everywhere
terrarium trope   in the middle   of nowhere
dismayed   in the district   of shadows
with grace   worn   light

crepe myrtle's winter shadow manifests
Fibonacci lesson on bar napkin
do death well   Sisters of Bon Secours
hither to unmarked grave-mate in captivity
& body pawned for mindfuck's hypocrite
sensualist hidden with Chekhov's gun

crisis meet hubris
just your usual sky-god-daddy fail
for stock ingénue longing to be femme fatale
our flesh dwelling in shared sadness
& damage control after hope
pitch perfected in paucity
Detroit's sound track made to fit
happy hour's poison caricature
of autonomous car
self aware & driving off cliff
riding shotgun
in patriarchy's scorched earth zoo
the animals remain

hand held shot of Shelley Winters
swaying with seaweed
mother omens & spiritual ascent
made longing manifest
flesh but a passing moment
our dwelling place for now

female gaze as damage control
after hope & utopia
transubstantiation
a kind of intermezzo
& peep show god cameo
with post mortem tongue-in-cheek
for Navajo cryptographer
decoding in camera obscura room
upside down & backwards

eau-de-vie

a fruit made better
with increate thirst perpetual
pearl born of antigen
envy of sublunar shadow
ardent weaning intermittingly faithful
& confounded by temporal mundane
dense & rare   fledgling's pleading
premonitions of flight
a shadow for a substance
a substance for a shadow
husk of flesh libation
& consummates flower

Corvus:
third eye stigmata

savoir sans connaître

for Marthe Reed

"We are only the temporary custodians of the particles which we are made of. They will go on to lead a future existence in the enormous universe that made them."

exquisite difference in cloaca kiss

nine times the feathers

in Tiresias' cap   (*for female caprice*)

bardo song throws Einstein's dice

carved from baculum: the most variable of bones

the hedgehog knows one big thing

but the fox knows all ye need to know

portent of null model's bower bird bet

with soothsayer slang for drinks

with the gods & the lost

blind & future

dead & electric

present & seeing

coalesced with dark blood

a mule has all the blue prints

to bring down the big house

matter tells space how to bend

& space tells matter how to move

black holes turn too

as stars they once were

spun before exploding

corvus stigmata

"Once organisms evolve the capacity for subjective evaluation, and the freedom of choice, then animals become agents in their own evolution. One of the hallmarks of autonomy, of course, is the freedom to mess up."

Richard O. Prum (*describing club-winged manakins.*)

all the clocks in grade school have cages
vibrating wing bone's road to decadent beauty
on the level every day with Mesozoic birds' raspy laugh
that poor little barfly didn't hear what you've said
she's waiting for the Corvalis kid till she's dead

happiness was upon us like a cult
funny if this was *it*
this was *everything*
avian decline in the metaphysical sense
beauty buys sweet obliteration
fin de siècle
in gathered fruit almost too ripe
burning beneath polymath pulse

I hope tomorrow is a fine day   (*it never is sir*)
long as the day is nothing   (*again*)
post coital socks & clairvoyant kids
our snakes transcend
seraph's status-quo-squid
summer lightening
quick & bright flashes in dark sea
past this cruise ship to nowhere

> **arrivée de toujours**
> **qui t'en iras partout**

Equus asinus X Equus caballus
our collective spirit ordained by decrepit mule
for boatman's miracle with despair indisposed
slap in the face with wound side up

Persian scribe take note
of boss-fix powdered baroness
exposed as hoochy-koochy dancer
& flatterer of meek animals

mechanical pianos & tin whistle
embody sybarite's splendorous dream
glitter of death & sweet scented decay
gives rise to singular reflections
never said

red sky in morning

for Joseph McTague

drink & live ravenously
marry two Marys
finely boned & almost immaculate
their gilded veins pulse with hindsight
all these "*wish I were here*" souvenirs
yields beacon in the company of lost souls
shod with horsehoes lodestones
wishbone breaks rabbit foot
fed on music fragments
illuminated under tabernacles & St. Sabastian lacerations

frothy gills formed our corporeal state
this crucible of meaning   convalescing everywhere
poaching it   so hard   in the architecture of plough
fetishizing a mule as bodhisattva
at dusk birds return again roosting fallow
perched on a doll's discolored hat & reborn in mud
swaddled in clouds
destiny without divining bird   staining auger sky
& enter realm of nonduality
it is not love   or not love   but loving invariably constantly

goldilock's zone

"In my lucid intervals
make a trip to drunk-land
with the Yellow Emperor,
and the Book- Debouchee…"
-Alice Notley
(1975- Alice Ordered Me To Be Made)

wampum seawant

a day gone like cigarettes

with blood brightly awake

some dopey saint

or decommissioned ship

moored & scuttled

my fifth rate frigate sunk

with requiem for late & soon

the perch of ethereal drunkards

waiting to sigh & die already

for next drink's seer

of what the owl left

untold want

spoils for the sullen
fainting sans couch
& knowing there are exactly
two kinds of thieves
the trick it seems
is to live by wit's
premonition forecasts
for the birds
by way of stolen stars
& self imposed rune

M _ _ Flower Hotel

portrait of a girl in glass
beneath a sign – missing two letters
on a balcony in Beirut
Mar Mer (*sea saint*)   draws last breath
past bitten lip moon   waning & thirsting
an indignity of flesh
for shameless shadow's
ache sheaved sacred
in hills beyond hearing
white sea anointed   betwixt harlot & prophet
serpent's scorn of necks never kissed
drinking light from eyes & crushing shells
to blaspheme humility with purple tombs
filled with jasmine shocked vessels
as coffins voluptuous scent   both too much & too little
moments we cease to mask
when seduced or wounded
in deafening quiet of ragged sublime
inchoate realm of the fedayeen beyond
fortress of bitter vetch
grown out of each seed & brick alike
these plants – that starved the world
as time stood still
in catacombs below

tanto y mas

for Megan

Si resucitará?
dawn broke lapsing into laughter
through thankga clouds in Havana
foaming wake swept up & drowned
with Mary's cranky crow & militant magpies
all five seasons in one day
"the problem is, we don't know what the fifth one is…"
water's dark refuge
for missed mermaid on horizon
all the way to Howth's golden ratio
& dives deeper still

'translation' from the Latin transferre   to bring over
trace back the steps   backward to home
replaced with vestigial fluency in language of postcolony's
craic & propensity for self destruction   painfully hybrid rapport
for schism of beloved   otherwhereness
body of other   notwithstanding
both tongue tied & loose   awoke & besotted
caprichos avail themselves   & cannot be helped
like wild beasts'   transmigration of souls
o rocks   *tell us in plain words*
she covers her head & uncovers her head
echolocation by way of veils

this & nothing else
exile your memory
to sing a hymn skywards
changing under fox mask
as the moon drifts four centimeters every year
our path is clear from the beginning
on rain festered shorelines
a jaded albatross waits on the *trá*
shrapnel in outstretched wing
in parallax pitch of angels' share
robbed by sublime dowry
of vixen shriek echoed on grey sea
with mother tongue bereft of banter
abounding cadence remembered
from lullaby by dint of melody
remnants of ruined disciples
in brightly lit threads
a sort of light-crown
for our thin skin reactions
under Victorian lingerie
armed to the teeth & all al dente
strutting Rumi references
but vanquished by amnesia peddler's
for cosmic mnemonic
mysteries that hide within light
the facilitator of gloaming in Glencree
says *Ireland doesn't have a golden hour*

it just goes from grey to black
& then toasts me from the other ditch
with translations of graffiti sheep
those beatific seekers

all ghosts wait like lovers
above coursing waters of grotto virgin
& tattered signs for missing girl
her photo faded on tree in Glencree
where I hope she lives still

mycorrhiza mockingbird

for Padraig O'Malley

the Irish call blue notes long
fungal filigree girdled by divine arms
here one minute & still here the next
torn from limb to nimbus
bare flowering stage
explodes from emptiness
in sometimes glorious overture
essentialist anti hero holds black parasol
against scalding sun
& shadow twin decays on rubble
the ghosts are his   defiance is hers
for doomed heroine within every tree
her body an effigy
in mockingbird aspirations
wearing heptapod wristwatch
piano tuned with memory decay
& the nature of daylight
each key congregating spirits that alight within
she can also dance adagio

erato's erratum

for Milton

la chanson du mal-aimé
feather harvest in the factory
as innocent as lightning
pruned back sleep boundary's
blight in sleepless night
& kept awake by mule
gilding my entrail guitar
no guts no glory for decay's
history of wings
weeping blood & fire
for selfies shot in pre-fab deceit
basic evolution remembered
in provenance of plastic
I'm a sucker for duplicity
& thinly veiled break-downs
under the breathy music
a dark shape opens up
to pupil proselytizing
translation of light appeased
to cure absolute evermore
flying in sainted blood
in our far-flung cells
encoded like fists kissed
in a modest scandal

marginal utility

cops shot another man
while you ate a paleo muffin
with shared burden of insomnia machine
& sommelier's artisanal wig

select emojii race option here
in gilded dream foretold by Kabuki
master's embryo embroidery of
cicadas born bone-colored in tree
sucking sap with punch drunk viragos
birthright to potential
obliteration   beautiful
as small deaths'   twin shadow
ours wait behind green patina door
knock-knock
who's there?   kitsuné
kitsuné who   in brick dusted placage
lies here

we are all sea-starved selkies
& excommunicated foxes
not through crime but favor
of the desire machine
unable to resist
exploited well and granted

little by little eyes
trained outward to sticker
priced life and displaced deceit
meandering under current
with sitcom-numb-laugh
and other third act issues
not imposed by gods or devils
but offering gifts most precious:
mules, ravens, & black cat bones

the heir of labors
fortune is a woman
manifesting revenge
for post agrarian shackle
domestic serf turned
nursing home meat bag
saints' and merchants' tombs
raise stammering truth from
a history of two worlds
lè marasa covered in blessing
& cursed in caul of sea born longing
you are your you
willy-nilly   here at all times
still waiting for a life
up there and it wanders away
all things must live in a light
of diminishing graves

only wilder
and more solitary
consecrated nest empty
unexplored and wrecked
booming singular
in warning pitch
rife in myriads
for dweller within
agrarian asphyxia
enter blessed muck and rot
swamp as sacred marrow
for changelings & wives
six cents on the dollar
thus the shore is shorn
and the trees hold it by right of possession
sooner worn out
so much for the night
a mere shadow
and reminiscence
in this hum of refuge
distant and uninquiring corpses lie more low
than our curiosity go
keels and anchors alike
faith of our kindred bird
bounding into buoyant light
on this broken horizon

ruins of a goddess' shrine

upon the heaps of fallen gods
kissing hems & avoiding eyes
child of dark hearted language
night twin in hematoma garment
crows nest in scarecrow hat
a crown mocking god & grain & the sky itself

more inclined to talk than sing
with claddagh caw as cuneiform rapture
vines sprout cursive message from petrified egg
forged in praxis perfect
kiss-bruised lip in frail twilight
serves as trial for virtuous devils
& other notes from the fertile crescent
scarified on tear swollen paper
laughing & weeping at once for hope of being found
like ants on the nose of an unwitting god
who murmurs in their sleep
for a name forgotten   (*her own*)
no end in you
these visions from exile
open your eyes backward
backchannel this whisper inward
as premise to foresight
sigh at cloudless sky

become ashes born in drouth
drunk djinns' sea breath
seeds the body infinite
concealed from the senses
blood is naught but
knows the blessed dead
are standing about you & watching

Tracey McTague is a dissident, poet and visual artist born and raised in Brooklyn, New York. She occupies a house on Battle Hill with her daughter Aurora Morrigan, and works for the Global Alliance of Muslims For Equality. Her secret home is in New Orleans.

ACKNOWLEDGEMENTS

Special thanks to Christopher Ando, who created the chapter seal homage to our mule, fox and raven brethren. And to Brendan Lorber for translating their light to the page. Much gratitude to Mike Joyce for creating the Little Red Songbook of Sphinxes cover; after the great Jane Teller and I visited Golub's sphinx at the Met Breuer. Labor rabble rouser Jeff Schioppa told me about the concept of marginal utility many years ago, and like all good corvids, I cached the shiny bit away for later. Grateful always for my friendship with the brilliant peacemaker Professor Padraig O'Malley. Forever indebted to Megan Burns for her spiritual vigilance and her tireless guidance as my publisher and friend. A deep saikeirei bow to the Maestro John Godfrey for his beautiful notes on an early manuscript and his ever inspired spirit in the struggle.

Trembling Pillow Press

I of the Storm by Bill Lavender
Olympia Street by Michael Ford
Ethereal Avalanche by Gina Ferrara
Transfixion by Bill Lavender
Downtown by Lee Meitzen Grue
SONG OF PRAISE   Homage To John Coltrane by John Sinclair
DESERT JOURNAL by ruth weiss
Aesthesia Balderdash by Kim Vodicka
SUPER NATURAL by Tracey McTague
I LOVE THIS AMERICAN WAY OF LIFE by Brett Evans
loaded arc by Laura Goldstein
Want for Lion by Paige Taggart
Trick Rider by Jen Tynes
May Apple Deep by Michael Sikkema
Gossamer Lid by Andrew Brezna
simple constructs for the lizzies by Lisa Cattrone
FILL: A Collection by Kate Schapira and Erika Howsare
Red of Split Water a burial rite by Lisa Donovan
CUNTRY by Kristin Sanders
Kids of the Black Hole by Marty Cain
Feelings by Lauren Ireland
If You Love Error So Love Zero by Stephanie Anderson
The Boneyard, The Birth Manual, A Burial: Investigations into the Heartland by Julia Madsen
You've Got A Pretty Hellmouth by Michael Sikkema
HEAD by Christine Kanownik
marginal utility by Tracey McTague

Forthcoming Titles:
Unoriginal Danger by Dominique Salas
Book of Levitatons by Anne Champion and Jenny Sadre-Orafai
Book of Monk by John Sinclair
It's Not A Lonely World by Erin M. Bertram

Trembling Pillow Press

Bob Kaufman Book Prize

2012: *Of Love & Capital* by Christopher Rizzo (Bernadette Mayer, judge)

2013: *Psalms for Dogs and Sorcerers* by Jen Coleman (Dara Wier, judge)

2014: *Natural Subjets* by Divya Victor (Anselm Berrigan, judge)

2015: *there are boxes and there is wanting* by Tessa Micaela Landreau-Grasmuck (Laura Mullen, judge)

2016 *orogeny* by Irène Mathieu (Megan Kaminski, judge)

Please visit tremblingpillowpress.com for details on our new book prize in honor of poet Marthe Reed.

www.ingramcontent.com/pod-product-compliance
Lightning Source LLC
Chambersburg PA
CBHW022117090426
42743CB00008B/897